MEDITATIONS ON RISING AND FALLING

T0163454

The Brittingham Prize in Poetry

MEDITATIONS ON RISING AND FALLING

Philip Pardi

The University of Wisconsin Press

The University of Wisconsin Press
1930 Monroe Street, 3rd Floor
Madison, Wisconsin 53711–2059

www.wisc.edu/wisconsinpress/

3 Henrietta Street
London WC2E 8LU, England

5   4   3   2   1

Printed in the United States of America

Library of Congress Cataloging-in-Publication Data

Pardi, Philip.
    Meditations on rising and falling / Philip Pardi.
        p. cm.—(Brittingham prize in poetry, 2008.)
    Poems.
    ISBN 0-299-22730-8 (cloth : alk. paper)
    ISBN 0-299-22734-0 (pbk. : alk. paper)
    I. Title.
PS3616.A735M43   2008
811'.6—dc22   2007039956

For Carolyn and Emilio

CONTENTS

ACKNOWLEDGMENTS

Many thanks to the editors of the following journals, where some of these poems first appeared, sometimes in earlier versions or under different titles: *AGNI (online):* excerpts from "Seventeen Wings"; *Chronogram:* "Just Outside Utopia, Texas"; *Exile: The Literary Quarterly:* "God's Shins"; *Gettysburg Review:* "Drinking With My Father In London" and "Leaving Angelo"; *Hotel Amerika:* "Seven Parables of the Return"; *Indiana Review:* "Angels With Headaches"; *Marlboro Review:* "Two Hands"; *Mid-American Review:* "Three Meditations" and "Here"; *New Orleans Review:* "Poem Without Birds"; *Nimrod:* "Call and Response"; *Painted Bride Quarterly:* "Sonata"; *Texas Observer:* "Bracing Myself to Hear the Day's News."

"Bracing Myself to Hear the Day's News" was reprinted in *Is This Forever Or What?: Poems and Paintings From* Texas, published by Greenwillow Books.

I am indebted to everyone at the Michener Center for Writers for their generous support and many kindnesses during my time at the University of Texas at Austin. Heartfelt thanks to Susan Briante, Darin Ciccotelli, Maria Hong, Judith Kroll, Khaled Mattawa, Farid Matuk, Bruce Snider, Sam Taylor, David Wevill, and Abe Louise Young for lending ear and eye to early drafts of this manuscript. Special thanks to Steve Gehrke for his persistent and patient assistance. I'm sincerely grateful to my family for support and to Dave Costabile, Jenny Langsam, Holly Reinhorn, Steve Webber, and Rainn Wilson for decades of friendship and encouragement.

I.

Here

Then one day it happens: two birds
flying from point A to point B

>fall in love with the idea of point C.
>No wind but what's winged into being.

On this they rise. Below them, small
as mustard seeds, whales and narwhals

>roll to show their bellies, and if I lower
>this pencil, the birds are liable to chase

such whiteness. On and on they fly, over
water, for a lifetime and a half, beating

>*swords* into *words*, *words* into *ords*,
>to where I write with a pencil made

of birdseed.

Drinking with My Father in London

With his mate, Wilfred, who was dying,
I discussed ornithology as best I could
given the circumstances, my father flushed
and silent, a second pint before me,
my fish and chips not yet in sight.
Condensation covered the windows
and in the corner a couple played
tic-tac-toe with their fingers.
Behind it all, convincingly, the rain fell.
The mystery, Wilfred was saying, *isn't flight.*
Flight is easy, he says, lifting his cap, *but*
landing—he tosses it at the coat rack—
landing is the miracle. Would you believe
thirty feet away the cap hits
and softly takes in the lone bare peg?
Would you believe no one but me notices?
I'd like to come back as a bird,
Wilfred says, both hands on the glass
before him, and here my father
comes to life. *You already*
were a bird once,
Wilfred, he says, *next time,*
next time you get to be
the whole damn flock.

Leaving Angelo

How long, he says, does it take, he says,
to drive? Four days, I say, seven states.

I always liked, he says, a drive, he says,
his every sentence incised by commas

of air begged off thin blue tubes. Once, we
drove, he says, to Florida. So many,

so many, dead deer, but beautiful, the trees!
By the window, his lover holds

his own hand. The hum of hospital
voices continues its slender recital

as we watch Angelo breathe. He offers
a smile. Like here, he says, and nods

to the screen of odd parabolas
rising beside him. My dashboard, he says,

and this, he says, twitching his nose
so the tubes are raised in relief, this

is the wind in my face. The horror
of how we go on. Near

Philly a fan belt snaps, we lose
two days. In a Motel 6 in Arkansas,

my son takes his first fertile steps.
Home again after seven days

an answering machine awaits
alive with lights.

The Roofers

Bare backs glistening like wet stones, they stand
bowed and hammer-swinging. To say they're tanned

is dead wrong. A uniform is what it is,
plus jeans and boots, plus weight. Each bears his

sweat in a different way. For example, the one
who, in a few moments, will fall, is having fun

with a fly he's freed from a roll of tar paper.
You've come five hundred miles and now you're

here, Amigo, he says. *You're farther from home*
than I, Chico, and I'm farther from home

than I ever thought possible. All this time,
an old radio has been playing. All this time,

the cambered shift of shingles to shoulders that know
the heft of sixty pounds. And when the radio

starts its slow slide from ridge-top to drip-edge,
when it slips and flips and kicks and falls to the hedge

below, they laugh, to a man they laugh, but the man
who'll fall laughs least. Perhaps in his gut he can

feel that gutter giving way beneath him,
or perhaps the radio was his. Or perhaps, in some dim

nod to weight's habit of tending to stillness,
his one great still act is to witness

what will come and where it will come from.
For years, he's said: *He's working, he can't come*

home for a phone call, Mamá. He pauses now,
wrist to brow, eyes closed, not thinking of how

it got to be this way but when, when
did that lapse linger? If his friends ask, then

he tells them straight out: *My brother was killed,*
killed. But every Sunday, his heart filled

with shame, he hears the same soft phrase:
You're taking care of your brother? And each time he says

yes. Each time he says yes: *It's just, he's working*
today, Mamá, he's working hard, he's making

good money. Sundays pass. His mother hears
of girlfriends, raises, and a new used car, tears

in her eyes as her oldest recounts it all. But mostly
he works. It's been two years of long days he

spends working hard enough to send back home
what two good sons should send back home,

and when it's time for him to fall, he's facing
not down but up, away from what is racing

up to meet him, and into a song that lifts him
not high, not far, but back to the twoness of them.

After Peach Season

We move through the world, we divide the world.
We expect, then we see, each act of sight

a slight reworking, an exacting, each
glance a guess at what and whom. We stare down
that crooked line between seeing and seeking

and dammit if we aren't surprised sometimes.
And so, driving west, perhaps, in search of

trees grown heavy, we expect to find trees
grown heavy, but find instead the moment
after sweetness: peaches, sweet peaches that

have fallen to an earthy still, and *click*
the moment clicks shut. Isn't there beauty

in that, in those hands that can toss one hunch
after another into baskets, bruiseless,
as if peaches could be found at any

time of year? What then is the worth of peaches
after hands have failed to rein them in, failed

(if we're to speak of prices) to land them
in the wicker of watery mouths? We
venture out in search of something framed

by the sky, small words our best levers
for what we fully intend to pluck,

and it's then we see what wasn't foreseen:
that peaches, to be peaches, will fall. And we
in turn can only hope that if when we

went off to find them they had yet to fall,
when we arrive they will have yet to land.

Sonata

From our small balcony
I watch you come near, arms
about a burlap sack bearing
the full spectrum of fruit,
                              watch
as you pause on the baker's stoop,
                                        note
how he makes you laugh
deep from your knees,
                          think
I must learn how he does that.

Early afternoon, early autumn, late
in my youth
I find myself seaside,
                          salt
on the apple I bring when we walk,
                                    whole moments
when the world is louder than my thinking
about the world.

Let us thank God for noise.

We've come to a place where I cannot name the birds
and because I look constantly
                                  for tanagers (scarlet

or hepatic) here where they have no reason to be,
I see them constantly,
                              mistakenly
in olive groves, small fig trees, in swift scattered dispersal.

                    Those who fear joy
will be found by it,
a ragged pothole of honey
                              and cinnamon
suddenly underfoot,
                              unfathomable thud

of things not meant to fly
                              landing.

Things taking their place with a vengeance.

              *

On the train, riding back to the city
(any city will do, any train)

the trees and village walls have been wiped clean.
Rain and an easterly (westerly) wind

darken all, and the windows are no match.
The mind has shown itself, the question is

do we like what we see? (Can we praise our
praising?) The sea, yes, and beside the sea,

a town, and when it rained we'd close the blinds,
leave the windows open, and undress. And

how I prayed for rain, saw it coming
in even slimmest clouds. Even now

I know it's near, just beyond the fast
horizon, eighteen miles away and closing.

*

He fears falling and all he sees is height and the craning of necks. Still, even in falling there is order. We fall *down*, after all, which gives us what we fear. We drop as vultures rise, embracing what is offered.

Here are the broken ladders from which workers fell, to which they never returned. Here is the poison ivy into which they fell. Here is the poison ivy into which their sons fell. Here is what jarringly falling is, with no time landing to prepare for—

We prefer the noise we know, the known ways of drawing quarter moons over orchards sleeping. We find a joy we knew not to look for in a place we swear we've been. Those who fear it will find its skin easy to pierce as cherry skins, will find too late there's no place to hide stained hands.

Looking for more, you smell it, turning, you hear it, the only thing between it and you: a yellow-throated thing the size of a phoebe keeping a branch between it and you as it moves through the hemlocks. The small defeats are small. The small victories are victories. The way a wren seems to have wings, not be wings.

Under the overpass, a broken pigeon has lain for weeks. The calm and patient eaters have come and gone, flesh is elsewhere flesh again, body reduced to bone, but clinging, still, to feathers.

*

The sea, and beside the sea, a town, and
above the sea, diving, brown pelicans,
and above it all, a small balcony

and one man falling, falling, sipping his tea,
awaiting the footsteps he knows. Meanwhile,

he watches a scene unfold on the quay.
A boat unloads its nets, the men struggle
with the weight of what's inside (here he turns
to look but the alley is empty). It
looks for all the world like wings, but vast,

the tips caught in the tangles of wet knots,
barbs on end like sharp-finned backs, caught
and caught again. Because he doesn't speak
the language of such things, such things don't
speak to him. He watches as the men work

to free the wings (if they are wings) then checks
again for her approaching steps, then back
quick to these men whose hands and words he can't
fathom. And yet he knows shout from salute,
jostle from jeer, just as he knows finches

from kingfishers. He knows that she'll arrive
out of breath from the steps, and then she'll add
change to the jar they save for wine. Perhaps
she's bought wine so the coins will clink loudly
to the bottom, or perhaps (he turns

again and still no sign) (the wings are now
out of sight behind a crowd of sailors,
hawkers and wives) (if they were wings they were
huge, but if they were huge how could they
be wings?) he thinks perhaps he ought to close

his eyes against it all. The moment
before joy is horizonless. What falls
falls surrounded by what's falling. Too late
the fear of landing, too late. She's near.
From the quay, the first slight scatterings.

Two Hands

1.

We don't, in truth, prepare
adequately, competently
even,

for this. The letter
that arrives or, eventually,
doesn't,

the doorbell unfingered
still. The word un-
unfurled. We learn

from what we fear to run,
but this—what nothing
taught us the way

away from—runs with us.
With, a word we once loved.
The jacket we first slip

out of, then fold before the railing,
the finches building, even
as the island is sinking,

their nests.
We each must make our peace
with what is evident

though mistakes are made—
fearing you've misplaced
God, you decide you might

have been misplaced, might
be about to be scooped
into arms, blue and up.

2.

I know, if there's meaning,
it isn't here, in what
my hands—so cold

in the a.m.—can grasp,
though I know, too, you can't
keep a thing from meaning,

having tried, having seen
others try, having held
and in the end withheld

what I thought
was there.
For their sake, then, I drink

warm tea, that
they have a warmth
to which to cling. What

I found, I found unhidden,
if we can speak
of finding what's in plain view,

the fly's epistemology
of circle, touch, and taste,
and ours, however impious, of

stumbling onto, or
running into, or
sitting accidentally upon, or

reaching, before
knowing what—now
airborne—was tossed.

3.

The end, I said, was near, but still
we climbed toward it, unsure
how we came to be

so far below—each of us
a castle built of time, assembling,
between first and last, our own

history of touch. Who will you be
when your heart and fists
disagree, everything warming

everything, certain your Spanish
has failed you, asking to have it
explained again, the story

of the woman who, before
the war was even over, married
the sergeant who'd tortured her? Climbing,

the way is lined with those
who turned aside, which
is a thing joy does to you,

but this is different, you want
to believe, this is how
what wants you, what you,

in fact, say you want, may not
in the end come clean. Each touch
a blessing, though you would not

be blessed by anything
that would distinguish blessed
from unblessed.

4.

Stopping now, midstep,
the idea upon him
that this is no time not to be

praying, he steps aside, assumes
the posture of the closed-eyed,
prays, though

to look at him, fingers pressed
to nose bridge, you'd think first
of a headache, second

of grief, and third of the way
we strain to recall
even the name, sometimes,

of a loved one—and such is his luck
that, from nearby,
he hears a reply, a bell

ding-dinged slightly, as if
just for him, as if
there weren't, just then,

two men cleaning the belfry,
a mop handle falling
and bouncing against the rim

as the workers, out of sight
briefly in their cold upper reach, share
a cigarette, having

mopped themselves up the stairs
and into a corner, though neither
admits, later, to a mop falling.

5.

Late in my desire for you
but early
in my thinking about my desire

for you—I'm nothing
if not slow—I watched you watch
the lake

the quiet neck of the heron
the rower
whose oars moved

like wooden spoons
through soup—
you were quenched

the way thirst can be quenched
so quickly
whereas I found a hunger

that would require months
of patient feeding—
when you turned to walk ahead

I held tight
thinking
what the hands lose

is for the eyes to find
and what the eyes lose
is for the heart to find

but the heart
when it loses a thing
is left to fend for itself.

6.

—Time, Sir, bleeds, and ours
are wounds
that are stopped

for years. For years
we press hard
and it's surprising, this

habit, if that's what
it is, of using two hands
where one will do.

This flowing which is in us
is us—hear
how it rasps, sings,

even, not with
but toward its own kind
of staying: *and this, and*

this, and this
it whispers.
How we long for a stay.

How we long to free one hand,
only to realize
one is half of what's needed

to pray, and then, working,
gradually, the other free,
we're left

with only the fact
of our hands, with how
it's *to* them we should pray.

7.

The mirror, which you love
for having remained, since
childhood, cool

to the cheek, which flips you left
to right, can't,
however much it tries,

lift feet
to brow, can know nothing
of ascent

but what it sees
and immediately forgets.
For you, the way up is marked

by the way we move
through it, the hands grasping
what soon the feet will step to, past

grackles twirling like kites
but without the strings
to untangle afterwards

and the boy cutting each one loose
save his favorite, which he fastens
to a park bench, leaves aloft,

into the night, with a wind
that seems to aim for it alone—how
like a tree after emptying

the world then seems—between risen
and fallen
what, in place, remains.

Poem Without Birds

Yes, there is a blue sky above,
beneath which

the diviners

look up. Oncology
of clouds,

disgust

in the wind, twigs
and wrappers

waiting, waiting.

A student sleeps in the grass
as a squirrel absconds
one by one with her peanut M&Ms.

So many ways to avoid the central fact.

At bus stops, lacing boots,
beneath spotless statues,

the posing

above which we find ourselves
looking down

for proof the clouds have passed.

II.

God's Shins

I need a watch, Don Pedro tells me, because sometimes it's cloudy.

At the construction site, a dashed white line on tarmac tells of wires overhead. A machine operator, looking down, is reminded of what is above, just as the botanist, dead pond before him, might see holes in the largest of fabrics. At the door to a hospital room, an old friend shakes her head, can't bring herself to approach my grandfather. We watch him sleep with a sleepless face. *He was such a good dancer*, she says.

Yes, a man explained to me, the kite is like the soul. The strings are long or short. Some, belonging to the prophets, seem endless. When the wind dies down, each returns to its home, and as we coil the string around our fingers, we vow never to let it stray so far again.

Don Pedro draws near a grackle that stands its ground atop an upturned wheelbarrow. *Finders keepers*, says the bird. *Isn't that what you've been trying to teach me all these years?* I watch man address bird. *Last night I dreamt of a world without stillness*, he says. *And it was such a still world! So still, there was no word for go, no verbs, nor any hope for flight, for flight was all around us.* At this, the bird wept.

Some days I'm an *I*, occasionally a *you*, but most days I'm a *he*.

I want to tell you about my grandma, how she taught me the difference between a slider and a curveball in her kitchen, fingers tight around a grapefruit, how one night when a player went down looking with a man on third she explained, *It's because his wife is due to have twins any second!*

You think you're alone but upstairs a neighbor is watching through raised blinds. If you pick your nose, it's for her. If you look up, you rehearse the most cautious form of prayer: *Lord, don't do anything, but be near.* It could be her son started school today, or her marriage is ending, or both. What she sees in you is mostly a matter of shoes left behind like an echo of feet.

At night, beetles come close, bless Don Pedro's thighs, calves, and shins. In his dreams, a lover unwraps her self from his, a little on the left, a little on the right, like tight apparel being worked off, making her way to the soles of his feet from which she falls through the floor and out of his dreams. What touches blesses. Don't reach for it.

Touch my hand when I'm lying there. If I can, I'll give you a sign, some indication, to prove you're wrong. You must keep your eyes peeled for even the smallest hint.

I did touch his hand. It was cold, a tortoise shell.

But later, walking home, I saw signs. Sprinklers on in the slight rain. The bus driver singing to himself. The joy of pausing in one's steps.

In anticipation of a hug, he would remove the sunglasses from his breast pocket.

The man with the clipboard calls him over, calls to the boy who will translate. Business is slow, says the man, and the boy, translating, says: *Don Pedro, you know what's coming. The bastards!* You've been a good worker for me. *For him and his father,* says the boy, and then: *Don Pedro, you should just walk away right now, don't let him put you in the fields.* But these young men, they work hard, says the man, harder even than me, ha, ha, ha. You understand. Of course, there's always work in the fields, he says. Don Pedro considers the position of the sun: break time, he thinks. *Should we burn down the farm?* asks the boy.

Let x = yes. Then the answer is x.

I had come to suspect all things of holiness. The Braille of bird tracks, for instance, and the man lifting concrete blocks into a dumpster. But what about traffic? Or the senator who never speaks to his doorman—what part of that equation is holy? The senator walking too quickly from door to hand-held door? His unspoken words? Or perhaps the quiet doorman himself, who tells his wife: *El día que me hable es el día que le pego.*

Dusk. Father says: There's a gaggle of geese following us! Or are those dots of dirt on the rear window?

Mother thinks: Since when is desire dished out in such small servings?

The child asleep in the back seat asks nothing, but years later, retracing this same path, will wonder: When did I first notice the way light lifts all things just high enough to break them when dropped?

Some mornings, Don Pedro decides, the birds bring joy. But mostly it's joy that brings the birds.

That we'll be greeted by silence isn't the question. The question is, with what will we greet this silence?

The first morning mouthful of coffee is the best. That rare case of *YES* followed by *yes*.

I met the sage in Central Park. He was tired, holding one hand in the other. "I've been flying kites all day," he said. "I fly them high, hoping to give God a knock in the shins, make Him spill His tea and notice us." But the sages disagree on when God looked away. My Aunt Emily in Boston, for instance, says, "If Beethoven could go deaf, then surely God was snoozing. And World War I and II. He must have nodded off before Judge Thayer and Auschwitz and Hiroshima. But how then do you explain Ted Williams?"

When the crop duster disappeared, the farmworkers breathed again, and no one moved until Don Pedro moved. They followed him out of the fields to the packing shed where the man with the clipboard waited. The air was sweet, alive with things settling. Don Pedro pointed to his shirt and the man was silent. Don Pedro removed his shirt, sniffed it, held it out to the man, who leaned close but wouldn't take it. *Agua,* said the man with the clipboard. And Don Pedro, because he didn't know the word for chlorpyrifos, said: *Veneno.*

Amidst it all, one still bird, unmoved even by the screaming of saints.

Always with a reason—an empty glass, a window too far ajar, quick retrieval of a book—but each time it's the same: the father's eyes ease into the half-dark, the thing to be done forgotten until he's checked for the rise and fall, each rise and fall a yes, and always, on the way out, he needs to stop and go back for the thing, lest someone ask him where he's been.

In the end it was a matter of something more than a sound but less than a syllable.

Now the fields are burning. Row after row of cilantro, clover, and big-hearted garlic heads curl close to the earth. Red-green pepper fingers too bright to behold. Prayer, bow, surrender. The history of the world is the history of a body moving against its will, then replying. Always one no, or many, then a yes.

Just once the answer was yes, and that was the answer he believed.

What he learned as the fire raged was this: There is no remedy for no water but water.

Look, look, look, he said, there it is, the moment is changed, but at no time is change a moment. It slips in between, a star seen best when you look to one side.

The continent was moving, taking trees and wasps and our bedsides with it. We awoke one morning to find the constellations shredded, limbs severed, eyes pinned to thighs. The Pleiades were on the verge of spelling a word. It was then we realized we're the opposite of spilling: an unpouring. Soon there were bended knees inside each weary back. Silence of palms, a meeting of makers.

One morning, Don Pedro came to understand there is no distance like the lack of it.

"He says NO! in thunder; but the devil himself cannot make him say yes. For all men who say yes, lie; and all men who say *no*—why, they are in the happy condition of judicious, unencumbered travelers in Europe; they cross the frontiers into Eternity with nothing but a carpet-bag—that is to say, the Ego. Whereas those *yes*-gentry, they travel with heaps of baggage, and damn them! they will never get through the Custom House."

He noticed with satisfaction that his friend's wife had gained weight.

Tonight, the uneven darkness is equal parts bold and apologetic. It's the shabby moonlight epiphanies are made for, but I'm not due for an epiphany. I'm due for something lower in my body, something akin to the warming of hands by a mug of something hot.

The farmworkers turn away, ride their bikes into town, stand in long lines at payphones. Says Lucio: *I respect a vegetable that knows how to burn, lettuce isn't for me. Once in my town there was a fire at the plantation and for three days the whole valley smelled of coffee, everything smelled of coffee: your bed, your lover, your lover's sweat.* Later, Manuel tells me how he last saw Don Pedro: shirtless, sitting nearly cross-legged, drinking Mountain Dew, singing: *estoy sentado aquí, estoy sentado aquí . . .*

III.

Angels with Headaches

It's surprisingly hard for angels to get their hands on aspirin. Paperwork must be completed, explanations provided. Each morning, a long line winds away from the window in question. And if you could stand there, as I have, what you'd see is the pain of landing. Curiously, it's the head that reels from impact, even as the ankles burn. The earth is always harder than I'm expecting, one says. Another: It's just, after all that flying, I get carried away by the proximity of touch. And a third, who is perhaps more honest, says: I had my eyes closed the whole way down—I had no idea I could get so close, so fast.

*

To live here is a perpetual hiding. Waiting for the light to change, standing like any other in the early shadows, as far from home as is possible, she thought: I can't even tell who among the others is like me. Some move too fast, some too slow, and the ones in between seem lost. When the light signaled her to walk one way, she turned and stood as if to walk the other, and gradually the day passed. She became aware of a three-fold beat inside her: head-ankle-heart, head-ankle-heart. All day she stood there, and all day she saw the same thing: people coming and going in every direction. Every now and then there would be an exclamation, she later explained to me: They look up, always they look up, but all they see are birds.

*

All this time I've been afraid to return. I pass the days talking with the ones standing in line. I bring them water, save their spots while they pee. In the evenings, I make maps of where each one has been, and I plan my visit. I am no different from others. My desire thrills me such that it scares me a little. The look in the eyes of angels after they've made that first trip is filled with what they'll never again contain, a thing only expectancy can bear. On the maps on my wall, blank spots are emerging. I fall asleep eyeing what is not known being hewn from what is.

Three Meditations

1. Meditation on the Ego

Three sounds descending must land
even if the mind wrinkles to catch them.
Already alive, they are reborn.

Let me tell you about the ego, they say: Imagine
pages, loose and scattered, the reader stepping
from one to the next, at times over a great distance,

cobbling together a sequence, the wind revealing
flipsides with graphs or maps, page numbers
in cuneiform.

The ego is the part of you that fails to notice
birds
are watching.

2. Meditation on Rising and Falling

He saw the sky, empurpled on its way to blue, and considered pointing it out to others. But the moment was gone before a finger could unfold. So it is with God, he thought: gone before you can get the words out.

*

Walking, he considers how everything, even walking, lifts us up and down.

*

In the space where each year a leaf returns, an absence.
Nothing to bend low beneath an early snow.
Nothing to prompt the word *susurration*.
Still, in that place, a thing wants to fall
but can't.
Nothing but a voice: *with what*, it asks, *with what?*

*

Last night, the storm punctuated the lawn with laundry. Each wet white sock a comma as he paused to pick it up, back bending and unbending with care. Then, stopping suddenly, he slipped, fell hard, landed face up. Above him, the storm having passed, a single star. He thought: after a storm, stars appear. (No, let's not kid ourselves—

*

the line came first. Sitting at my desk, I thought: after a storm, stars appear. There were no socks, no wet commas.

Just the bright and wind-ripped world, then my tea grown cold. The truth never follows the comma. The truth *is* the comma.) We spin, and our spinning fills us with stillness: two bowls, each emptying into the other.

*

Sipping tea,
all is tea.

Sipping all,
all is lost.

*

He saw a falcon fly low, tap its shadow, then whirl away. So it is with words, he thought: gone before God can hear you out.

*

One tree avid with wind,
the tree beside it still.

We slide until we slip
into place, and all we do

is a settling after a stirring.
We've forsaken speed,

its gospel of dispersal.
Our walking is a too-patient

seeming: treasure found,
the way home lost.

*

The magician's trick was to pull a rabbit out of an empty top hat while perched high on the high wire. Night after night he did it, week after week, and when the acrobats went netless he was happy to go along. He never looked down anyway, and the rabbits were, as a rule, calm. Then one night, distracted by a woman with a fur lapel, he misspoke the spell, and out of his hat came a lion. And the weight, needless to say, was too great, to say nothing of imbalance, and both fell. In the time it takes to fall there's time, if you're quick, for just one spell. Everyone saw it. Inches above the sawdust, lion unfolded into falcon, left its shadow unrequited.

> *

It was here
before us

now it is
here before us.

> *

In place of a leaf, an absence.
Autumnal drool, slow slide from unevenness
                                        to un-unevenness.
A thing that must break
                    is bending.

In truth there are just three seasons—
                    rising, falling,
and incandescence.

Try. Try falling when it's your turn to float.

3. Meditation on the Left Side of a Chevy

Cars collide: a simple pop and the world is complete. Before and after, the same fanfare. In between, a fury of folding: calyx of body caught resisting what it used to rejoice in.

*

Stepping to the window, I see pigeon shadows tapping telephone poles, one after another, the way *massage* follows *massacre* in the dictionary. Two starlings look down from their wire, see the future, look up.

*

The tails of birds insist
                    we're here
to stay.
            Sirens arrive, unwind,
say: *It ain't so.*

*

The fact that sirens sound like wailing has been noted. That wailing sounds the same in every language, noted. That a pebble aches to shatter glass, conspires to catch
            the eye—this requires study.

*

We need to talk, Phil, I need to tell you about something truly amazing that's happened. I replay the message, trying to place the voice. Who would talk to me about such a thing?

*

Later, walking, I see the car being lifted onto a flatbed, its left side shaped as if to mouth the word *beatify*. By evening, flare-dust scattered in the left shoulder. Overnight, erasure. In between, another story.

Seven Parables of the Return

Having been there before, he returned, only to find one step fewer than before. Squirrels curled like commas marked the way, light falling hard on the softness of smoke. The next time: one step fewer. And so it happened, until the moment in between had been discarded. Before flowing, a leveling, he thought. Before flowering, an eradication.

*

Everywhere he turns, it returns.

*

She'd left a trail of seeds along the way, but that was long ago. For years she's wondered which will be the first to go, birdsong or bird? When it's time for her to return, the seeds have sprouted, grown tall. What was cut into shade now colludes with it. She makes her way from tree to tree, slaloming.

*

Song of one who leaves:
I'll believe it when I see it.

Song of one who returns:
I'll believe it when I've seen it twice.

*

No tale, after all, tells of sages running. Running is left to us, and we run fastest when we're almost there. The girl, removing her shoes, the faster to run. The man, kneeling, the taller to appear before God. The fawn, learning not how to run, but when.

*

She wanted to be one who had returned but couldn't bring herself to leave.

*

He aspires to go through his day without making a fist. So easy, thinking of getting down, to get up. One morning he finds bears have left the birdfeeder twisted in the shape of a long-forgotten vowel. For weeks, finches arrive, hover in midair. What is that fluttery thing? he wonders. The thing that brings you home when even home has failed you?

Under Hemlocks

It's spring again, my pockets
flush again
with the wrong currency,
a moment under hemlocks
where edges end,
birds here louder
than the pain in my body:
another love song, I'm sure.
No petals, no fingers,
ragweed kicked clean.
What was beautiful
becomes endangered,
a map worn thin from folding,
and if there are bees' wings
in the honey, we'll lick
each spoon clean.

*

We were talking the other day
but no one believed.
Such a relief, waiting
for a *what*
that's never gaining.
Isn't that us, eyes

round as square pegs
eying round holes,
thinking
I've been here,
I know I've been
here, stood
where I now stand
hand raised to temple
in pain or recall.
Can I remember what is to come?

*

(Here a voice says *look up!*
I look up, wouldn't you?)

One leaf
too tired to fall
clings
and in its clinging waves
and in its waving wants
all it sees and will not have.
Things fail and having failed disperse.
Each snowstorm, a failure,
each season, each breath.
I come to a place
where the paths are worn and dry,
a moment you live and re-live
until the intersection between it
and you is barren.
All our prayers are answered,
I'm told, but sometimes
the answer is no.

Just Outside Utopia, Texas

Even the mourning doves
seem happy

and the man
buying beer

at 8 a.m.
all smiles

bottle in one hand
stein in the other

as he sets each down
then opens

to I wish I knew
which verse

his large-print
King James.

Bracing Myself to Hear the Day's News

This small toy horse
on the shelf
is all I'd take
if the leaves of drought were to fall
or a great voice ordered the river
to rise
and it did.
A child's eye is our only hope
and hand.
Draw a window
jump through
erase it from the other side.

Call and Response

Just one thing dreams of returning as itself: the hands.

*

Never mind winter will be mild.

Never mind the dumpster is forever spilling.

A squirrel prays to God the way God must sometimes pray
        to a squirrel: don't, don't, please, don't . . .

Flattened. The tail, quivering.

*

You may be surprised by the speed at which decisions
are made for you.

You'll be excused if, reaching down for what you want,
        you kick it
just out of reach.

What if you escape, but escape back
                                into this same garment?

A meeting at the crossroads of water and water.
Boots for excellently crossing small streams,

                                      urns for pouring.

What if it fits, the footsteps spaced perfectly for your stride?

        *

On the radio, a man hears "The Star-Spangled Banner" from
      Hanoi.
Chance of rain today: 100%.
Morning, perforation.
The way water embraces itself is the revelation.
The man thinks of thieves spooning honey onto roses,
           running razors into tea bags, of what he'll do
           when his last pair of shoes is wet through, why
           there's always something between him and his
           idea of what's missing.
Two flies, trapped between window and screen, froze
      overnight.
The Vietnamese military band plays the anthem perfectly.
The man never liked that song, never liked the word
      ramparts.
Perhaps, he thinks, there's a mathematical function we've
      yet to invent, the precise algebraic formulation of
      caressing.
Chance of rain today, 100%.
The way an eggshell hides its soul till the revelation shatters it
      is the revelation.
From his front step, the man eyes newspapers drowned
      on sidewalks: this he likes, the news as landscape.
He longs to do for his feet what prayer does for the hands.
On the road, he can't see it, but he knows one bus driver has
      just waved to another.

        *

Each year, in the autumn, we visit the old house. We meet the new owners, if they are new, and walk through the garden, if they let us. Perhaps a plant needs pruning, or the fence a nail. We talk with them, explain the way water can rise quickly from the culvert, show them the spring in the lower meadow. And then we broach the issue of ashes.

*

Rain, and the robins descend
and get to work,
or is this their joy, their rapture?

Wet leaves, wet stones, wet skin, I listen, am listened to.
A marsh hawk unfolds, white-rumped and listing
left, lifting itself into hackberry limbs.

There is nothing that is not falling from us,
nothing we do
that isn't a grabbing.

*

Sometimes, watching you
from afar
           the same urge
I feel amidst hemlocks
when a rare redstart comes near:
be still, raise eyes slowly
                     go over
each aspect of wing, throat, limb,
                         press it hard
into memory.

*

Beneath the hum
of delay

a hand gathers,

ungathers:
the ebb and flow of the I.

There's always one sound

taking its place
behind another,

always a small plane

circling, circling.
Beneath it all, trees

and elegies: *This*

is how it happens. First
you forget to be yourself.

Then you get used to it.

*

All these years I would see them and make a wish.
"Hawks for good luck," we used to say. But now you tell
me they're actually vultures. The head gives them away,
you say. What does it mean to wish on a vulture? Do you
think they—the ones I meant to pray to—knew what I
meant?

*

"When we behold a wide, turf-covered expanse,
we should remember that its smoothness is
mainly due to the inequalities
having been slowly leveled by worms.

It is a marvelous reflection that
the whole of the superficial mould over
any such expanse has passed, and will
again pass, every few years, through

the bodies of worms. The plough is one
of the most ancient and most valuable
of man's inventions; but long before
he existed the land was in fact regularly

ploughed, and still continues to be thus ploughed,
by earthworms."
                Thus Darwin, late in life, looked ahead.

IV.

Seventeen Wings

1.

Falling
is the given, rising
the flame to which we cling

one yes after the windfall of no.

Like other bodies, ours
will obtain a height, but the question
remains whether

by gliding down or by leaping and grasping—

2.

Standing at the window with my son
in my arms, we watch the stars
then the streetlights
toggle off, the day not here,

coming. The coin
in midflip, the foul ball arcing
out of play, then in.
My son leaning into me, wholly.

3.

Think of slender hands
for catching, of how hard
the wrists will work to break your fall.

Don't think of being born into flight.

Think, if you can, of grace
and hunger
as the arc of falling

not from but into.

4.

In the night, a cloud
of small winged things
called close by the streetlight,
and the bats, feasting.

Aprovechar in Spanish:
to take advantage of
but not in a bad way.
To delight in what was given.

5.

The balance
unbalanced
by being inside a body

as if the body were weight not lightness,
as if my son, young enough to laugh

whenever I laugh
on faith,
weren't also learning when to make a fist.

6.

One day, probably a Tuesday,
this thing we call
rising

will uncoil inside you

and it's then
you'll rediscover your hands
one over each wing

and let go.

7.

The birds, though they embody your idea of return,
don't. The spot beneath the eaves, empty for the first
time since you built this house, the mornings quiet. This
is what you can't teach your son: what is not found is
itself a finding, absence not presence what touches.

8.

Older: Look!

Younger: Where?

Older: There!

Younger: Up there?

Older: A hawk!

Younger: How can you tell?

Older: Look:

(Off):   *Keeeeer-r-r . . .*

9.

Each day we're granted glimpses,
glances—

the world that holds us
held in place

as it is
by what it isn't

an emptiness requisite
for any embrace.

10.

Each day (I say,
you see) a fall from Earth

to Earth, tiny
collisions giving me voice.

Like a twig
that drops

I'm silent
except on impact.

11.

The horse that is pure
will change course in midstream

if the heart says so
so how will you feed the heart?

You, *a lover of horses,*
in love with their soft heft

and God's little trick
of making us care.

12.

Younger: What's that?

Older: Oh, oh—

Younger: What is it?

Older: It's got golden cheeks—I've never seen one
             before.

Younger: Have I seen one of those before?

Older: No, never.

Younger: Should I be excited?

Older: Yes!

13.

Tomorrow a gem might be found, today I count tiny lives: two mourning doves, one pregnant spider, and a chipmunk on a rock in a crouch like a boxer. And somewhere, out of sight, a truck or plane ascending. We have a back that must bend for us to bow or touch the Earth, and if bending were easier, bowing would be something else again, something like holding your breath and counting. The day lays shattered into splinters of light, and what the crows cannot gather dusk arrives to smother with wet blankets and carry off. We watch as if watching could save us, but we ought to fear being a witness. We ought to know what a witness must do.

14.

We learn
and re-learn a place
wander the far reaches

our souls on kite strings
our bodies the taught finger

we delight when the map is wrong
or given new colors, speak then
our best lie: *ours.*

15.

Think of the sparrow
in the act of love
using his wings to perfection

of the gardener who watches
as he waits to retrieve his trowel

of the gardener's son
who'll see the eggs
devoured by squirrels.

16.

What's surprising
is that we're ever
surprised—

in every fist   a hand
for every two fists   one heart

the heart outnumbered always
you wonder what God
was thinking.

17.

For one day, my son can count to seventeen.
He finds seventeen of everything: fingers,
freight cars, books to be read at bedtime.

The fly we free from an empty pop bottle
has seventeen wings, and each of us

is seventeen years old. For dinner,
seventeen avocadoes. Everything
he can't imagine is seventeen miles away.

18.

The task of accounting
for emptiness
is given out each day

those who fail
come back empty-handed

it's those who
don't return
who succeed.

19.

The day comes when my son, reading this, wonders whose hands I mean to catch him, whose hands dropped him to begin with. (The heft of halting in midflight, as coffee, warming your hands, cools.) The day comes when you see the northern lights and know to close your eyes, the better to hear them. (Shadows will cling to the light without which they are nothing.) The day comes when our only sin is distinguishing, when a thing breaks inside us, but not in half, not cleanly—

NOTES

"After Peach Season" is for Marla Akin.

"Poem Without Birds" is for Jeff Hoffman.

"God's Shins"

> *El día que me hable es el día que le pego* —"the day he talks to me is the day I punch him."
>
> *Veneno* — "poison," a word commonly used by farmworkers for pesticides.
>
> *"He says NO! in thunder . . ."* —the entire stanza is quoted from Melville's letter to Hawthorne, April 16, 1851.
>
> *Estoy sentado aquí, estoy sentado aquí* —"I'm sitting here, I'm sitting here." Lyrics from a popular Mexican song.

"Bracing Myself to Hear The Day's News" is for Tanya Dragic.

"Call and Response"

> The quotation in Section X is from Charles Darwin's *The Formation of Vegetable Mould*, first published in 1881.

THE BRITTINGHAM PRIZE IN POETRY
Ronald Wallace, General Editor

Places/Everyone • Jim Daniels
C. K. Williams, Judge, 1985

Talking to Strangers • Patricia Dobler
Maxine Kumin, Judge, 1986

Saving the Young Men of Vienna • David Kirby
Mona Van Duyn, Judge, 1987

Pocket Sundial • Lisa Zeidner
Charles Wright, Judge, 1988

Slow Joy • Stephanie Marlis
Gerald Stern, Judge, 1989

Level Green • Judith Vollmer
Mary Oliver, Judge, 1990

Salt • Renée Ashley
Donald Finkel, Judge, 1991

Sweet Ruin • Tony Hoagland
Donald Justice, Judge 1992

The Red Virgin: A Poem of Simone Weil • Stephanie Strickland
Lisel Mueller, Judge, 1993

The Unbeliever • Lisa Lewis
Henry Taylor, Judge, 1994

Old and New Testaments • Lynn Powell
Carolyn Kizer, Judge, 1995

Brief Landing on the Earth's Surface • Juanita Brunk
Philip Levine, Judge, 1996

And Her Soul Out of Nothing • Olena Kalytiak Davis
Rita Dove, Judge, 1997

Bardo • Suzanne Paola
Donald Hall, Judge, 1998

A Field Guide to the Heavens • Frank X. Gaspar
Robert Bly, Judge, 1999

A Path between Houses • Greg Rappleye
Alicia Ostriker, Judge, 2000